The
BHAGAVADGITA
Conceals

BLUEROSE PUBLISHERS
India | U.K.

Copyright © Kanduri Prameela 2024

All rights reserved by author. No part of this publication may be reproduced, stored in a retrieval system or transmitted in any form or by any means, electronic, mechanical, photocopying, recording or otherwise, without the prior permission of the author. Although every precaution has been taken to verify the accuracy of the information contained herein, the publisher assumes no responsibility for any errors or omissions. No liability is assumed for damages that may result from the use of information contained within.

BlueRose Publishers takes no responsibility for any damages, losses, or liabilities that may arise from the use or misuse of the information, products, or services provided in this publication.

For permissions requests or inquiries regarding this publication,
please contact:

BLUEROSE PUBLISHERS
www.BlueRoseONE.com
info@bluerosepublishers.com
+91 8882 898 898
+4407342408967

ISBN: 978-93-6261-532-9

Cover design & Typesetting: Kanduri Prameela

First Edition: March 2024

Bhagavadgita Conceals

Written and edited
by
Mrs. K. Prameela M.A.B.ed
In Dedication
to
My Beloved Parents
Smt & Sri Jayanti Jogarao

Published by
Nexen Designs
Visakhapatnam
9290526746

Writer's Note

I dared to write this small book "Conceals of the Bhagavad Gita", which comprises of a little essence of the greatest universal, practical and scientific book, The Bhagavadgita, the celestial song sung by the lord himself. There are hundreds of books on Bhagavad Gita written by great seers like Adiguru Sankaracharya, Swami Vivekananda and many other intellectual eminent scholars and philosophists. It is said that Mahatma Gandhi always carried this sacred book and got solace from it. One book will have only one name or title or at the most two titles. But the Gita has eighteen names or titles. By that itself one can understand the greatness and the depth of this book. The Bhagavad-Gita is not a theoretical book but a practical book. It seems theoretical but it is a book in which there are solutions for all the problems faced by mankind not only in the past but also in the present as well as in the future. Such a great and practical book is not within the reach of children or students to inculcate the Norms as decreed by god in the Bhagavadgita. It is happy to note that the verses in the Gita are made to recite in some schools and at some places by the children. But in this work-a-day world, it would be more benefited if at least a little essence or the gist of the great book is understood by the children in schools and colleges as they are the ones who carry forward the ethics and culture and thereby try at least to keep up the credibility of the country and augment their life standards both morally and ethically. Happiest be the person who is blessed to inculcate in his life the practical part of the Gita. They will not be victims to any bad events in life but get the courage to face the circumstances whatever may be the consequences, without distracting from dharma or righteousness. Hence I have taken this small chance of writing this small book in a very simple language to be read by the present day students or people who are more than westernized in all aspects. It would enhance the character and would frame an idea to read the entire Gita with meaning in course of time.

I humbly pray to the lord Sri Krishna to forgive me for any mistakes that come across in the course of writing this book. I remain thankful and grateful to the lord for I think he has used me as an instrument to convey his message to the children. I submit myself at his holy feet. I trust that who so ever read this book will attain strength to lead a pious and balanced life like that of a drop of water on a lotus leaf with mental peace in the world and attain moksha in the end.

OM TAT SAT

Fore Word

Gita is an unfathomable ocean of knowledge and everything in nature and creation is within him. Lord Krishna, Avatar of Dwaparayuga, focussed in Bhagavad Gita that the individual person is the proprietor or master of the body. But krishna who is the super soul present in everyone's heart, is the supreme proprietor and supreme master of each and every individual body. As such if we concentrate on loving Krishna alone, then the universal love, unity and tranquility will be automatically realised and the whole world would be full of love and enthusiasm.

Smt. Prameela has done a laborious research and dedicated her entire capacity to produce the essence of Gita, useful to each and everyone. All the vital aspects of Gita essence, including equanimity have been depicted in a useful and lengthy exercise.

Her attempt is certainly an example for youngsters to go through parawise and get self love, strength and willpower useful to the society.

I wholeheartedly appreciate her narrative description of love and hatred and how to conquer the evils of the ward or individual person which is the essence of the Gita.

"Sarve Jana Sukhino Bhavantu."

Yenduri Krishna murthi
President
Sri Gita Prachara Samiti
Visakhapatnam

<u>Note</u>: *Religion/ Morals without Science is lame.*

Science without Religion/ Morals is blind.

Albert Einstein

BHAGAVADGITA CONCEALS

The eighteen names of the sacred book The Bhagavadgita are:-

- Gita
- Ganga
- Gayatri
- Sita
- Satya
- Saraswati
- Brahma Vidya
- Brahma Vahini
- Trisandhya
- Mukthagehini
- Ardhramatra
- Chidhanandi
- Bhavagni
- Bhavyanasini
- Chira
- Para
- Anantha
- Tathvagnanamanjiri

The names of the 18 chapters in the Bhagavadgita are:-

- Arjuna Vishada Yogam
- Sankhya Yoga
- Karma Yoga
- Gnana Yoga
- Karma Sanyasa Yoga
- Atma Samyama Yoga
- Vignana Yoga
- Akshara Parabrahma Yoga
- Raja Vidya Raja Guhya Yoga
- Vibhuti Yoga
- Viswa Roopa Sandarshana Yoga
- Bhakti Yoga
- Kshetra kshetra Vibhaga Yoga
- Guna Triya Vibhaga Yoga
- Purushottama Prapti Yoga
- Divasura Sampadvibhaga Yoga
- Shraddhatraya Vibhaga Yoga
- Moksha Sanyasa Yoga

BHAGAVADGITA CONCEALS

The Bhagavadgita is a Celestial Song sung by Lord Sri Krishna in the Kurukshetra Battle Field with the Pandavas on one side and the Kauravas on the other side. It consists of 18 chapters. Totally it consists of 701 verses. It has four themes that are Karma, Bhakthi, Gnana and Vairagya Yogas through which one can reach God or realize God. Our life is of great significance because, only we have the discretion power of the good and the bad and the right and the wrong. We should be thankful to god for giving us this great intellect and perseverence by which we can realise our own self and then attain self actualization. It is the ultimate goal of human life although he may lead a life of unparallel pleasures and prosperities. The place of the highest and the lowest is the same burial ground. Nay! A rich man cannot be buried in diamonds. So before reaching the final destiny as stated by god, we should try to achieve "Moksha", by which we can live even after death eternally. This moksha is easy to utter but it is not so easy to attain as it seems to be.

The master of the universe and the architect of Gita assured that he would give "Moksha" to his devotees who would come to Him for rescue leaving all the other dharmas.

First of all to know the real meaning of moksha, we should read this word in Sanskrit. The first syllable 'Moha' and the second syllable 'Ksha'. 'Moha' in Sanskrit means 'Desire'. 'Ksha' in Sanskrit means 'decease'. So, together it means, "The decease of the "desire". Again, desire means, desire for wealth, power, sex, all material prosperity, all material things. All these desires should be won. Lord Buddha proclaimed that desire is the root cause for all suffering. Only when we have a wish and it is not fulfilled, we brood over and over thinking of it and the various ways of achieving the desires. Again the inborn manly enemies Kama, Krodha, Lobha, Moha, Madam and Matsarya must be rooted out. This is also easy to preach but hard to practice.

Men, as said, are ruled by these six vices and to overcome these vices means, to lead the life of an ascetic. When the doors of the heart are closed for these petty things, then only the heart opens for the new beauty within the heart internally. We will know the already, always, ever pervading beauty within the heart. This beauty is the "Satchitananda". It is the permanent joy and peace.

This eternal peace and the various ways to reach the Absolute, is given in the "Gita" by the author himself. He stated the duties of a man in this changing world and the dharma to be adopted by which one can live peacefully and finally get salvation in the end. He assured to give moksha even if one reads a chapter, a padam, a verse, or a line of the Gita everyday. He also said that even by mere utterance, Nama smaranam of his holy name, he would give that "Ultimate Bliss". It would be worth to take the name of God as Mantra (ie- Om Namo Narayanaya, Om Namo Bhagavate Vasudevaya, Om Namah Sivaya) at least 12 times in the morning, 12 times after having bath and 12 times before going to sleep. It will work wonders and purify the thoughts.

The Bhagavad Gita uttered by the Lord himself is the pot of knowledge showing the path to the devotees to dive in that knowledge of 'Atma' and get salvation or moksha in that knowledge through that knowledge. In other words, it is the unparallel knowledge of the Upanishads and the Vedas to reach the Absolute or to realize himself. It teaches us how a man should live and also the rites and the duties that are to be observed by man.

Just as a cloth in an oil lamp burns and gives light, though the oil is dusty, so also man should shine with Absolute wisdom, though living in this world of maya. He must lead a life like that

of a drop of water on a lotus leaf. The drop on lotus leaf will shine as long as it is on the leaf and finally merge into the water when it falls down but dos not get attached to it. So also, though man lives on the earth amidst the materialistic world, he must live like the drop of water without getting attached to the world and finally merge in the Almighty like the drop of water that merges in the water and looses its identity. Just as the cloth absorbs the oil and burns leaving aside the dust, so also man should absorb only the knowledge of the Absolute and remain unattached to everything else so as to attain perfect perfection. He should know the unanimity of God, which means the same God or Chaitanya or unseen power that governs us or whatever name we may give or call, dwells in all beings, be it a Brahmin, Muslim, Christian, Hindu, a fly, a dog, a bee or an ant. The same was made known to Jagathguru, Adi Sankaracharya, when the lord

came in the guise of a Chandala, with dogs.

The Gita is entirely a problem solution theory. It discusses all the problems that arise not only for a time but for all times and all ages and the solution for the problems for one and all times. It is not only for one age but for all ages past, present and future. It tells the reader the easiest way of attaining salvation or moksha, without rebirth which is inevitable for the born. Chanting Gita saves a man from the gallows of the "Yama" and reaches one to the Pada Padmam of the Lord undoubtedly.

The Bhagavad gita is not a recitation theory but a practical theory. The way to lead life as ordained by god in the Gita is to be practised by man. By reciting the Gita, one will get the fruits of good works. He gets Punya, but he will not be relieved of the bondages and the birth and death cycle.

By practising the way to live the life as ordained in the Gita, one will be relieved of the bondages and thereby the cycle of birth and death. The Gita was preached to Arjuna in the midst of the battlefield when the hero Arjuna dropped his weapons and requested the lord to turn the chariot back. He

was carried away by the bondages like father, mother, brother, guru etc. All these are the earthly bondages or attachments with the world living in the world of objects. All these bondages are illusions. They are connected with the senses and give no way to raise to a higher plane than we are but go on creating problems over petty things and there by the mind looses the intellect. Arjuna fell at the feet of Madhava as a refugee to show him the right path so as to raise his mind above petty trifles and do his duty unattached. Not only Arjuna but all the humans are bound to be tied to the bondages and fall in a dilemma in performing the duties promptly never distracting from the dharma. Arjuna is only a representative for the entire humanity. His doubts and problems represent the problems of humanity. Problems maybe different from person to person but suffering and depression is the same. All the humans will have to prostrate before the Almighty to guide them in a proper direction in such times.

At this lord Krishna revealed the secrets of yoga of wisdom. He told that death is inevitable for all born and so also the karmas. The Atma or the inner self has no connection in anyway to the duals in life and does not respond. Yet if one sits without performing his actions as ordained, it will be a sin. For example, a small child is crawling towards fire and a person who sees that, doesn't respond to save the child, it is a sin on the part of the person and he is liable to be punished for not performing his duty. Having born in this world, god has given certain duties to be performed duly by all men. He said that no one can stay even a minute without performing the action, maybe physical, mental.

He proclaimed that he is the doer. He is the cause of the doer. He is the

effect of the doer. Totally it means he is the cause and the effect. He is the creator, the protector and the destroyer. One has to perform the duties engrossed to him without being bound by it which gives rise to the bondages. The words I, My, Mine are very likely to beget bondages with the

physical and materialistic world. One has to perform actions without desiring for the fruits. Man has the right only to act but not to its fruits. (Karmanyevadhikaraste, maphaleshu kadachana) All actions, whether good or evil will have reactions which are the fruits, as Newton's 3rd law states that every action will have equal and opposite reactions. He is the giver of the fruits according to our karma. He gives not what we desire but only what we deserve. Whatever he gives, one must accept as the Prasad of god, it may be success or failure. Secondly, man is mortal. He cannot live more than the span given by god. One must be ready to face the death with courage. One can do it when one performs his duties duly and righteously as ordained by god. One has to discharge his duties and responsibilities without getting attached to the success or failures which are bound to give happiness or misery. One must detach himself from the feeling that he is the cause of the success and without he, doing the work, it will not be accomplished. On the contrary, one must feel that he has been an instrument in the hands of god to make the work a success. One can experience that when the feeling or thought of "I" is vanished. Then the life will be at peace. Man cannot stay even a second without doing karmas or actions. The actions are bound with the nature and the senses and hence one has to perform actions to live, to survive and to perpetuate. First of all the thoughts must be good. Every action comes out of motto which is the thought in the mind. That is the motto behind the action. So every thought must be good so that every action will certainly be good. Those good actions must be submitted to god. Then no one can anticipate reciprocal.

One has to perform the actions as worship and offering to God so that each action will attain divinity. No one can do bad actions as they cannot be offered to god just like rotten flowers that cannot be adorned to God. God is the giver of everything. We cannot give anything to God except a pure and devoted heart. He doesn't want gifts of pomp and splendor. He accepts a leaf, a flower, a fruit or a drop of water which the devotees offer with pure heart. The same was proved in Sri Krishnathulabaram when Rukmini devi equaled or balanced the weight of lord with small tulasi leaves whereas Satyabhama could not weigh the lord with her entire property of gold and rubies.

Man must come out of the clutches of dualities. According to the lord, men are divided into three categories basing on their gunas or qualities or natures by birth. They are Sathwikk, Rajasik and Thamasik. The Thamasik natured people are very lazy, arrogant, self centered, too short tempered and out of control of senses they will commit any sin and will not stop at anything to achieve what they want. They are not God fearing men and have no moral values. The Rajasik people always think too much of themselves and perform actions to beget name and fame. They feel too proud of themselves and think that the works have been accomplished only because of them. The Sathwikk people are soft and gentle and virtuous. They are Godfearing people. They

fear to commit any wrong or mistake. Hence, man must stick to satwikk nature. One must be kind in words, kind in deeds, kind in heart, ready to help others, be compassionate to fellow beings whoever he may be, be devoted to the lord, eat soft and easy food which will develop intellectual abilities and above all have trust in god and the dharma that is ordained by God. One must stick to righteousness at any cost whatever the consequences may be. One must leave the petty responses over trifle things that happen in day to day life. One must realize that He is that imperishable Atma which is the Adyatma, Adibhuta and the Adidaiva. One must realize that all beings dwell in Him and he does not dwell in anyone. He upholds all the beings and cherishes them and at the end all beings merge in him to bring forth the next cycle of evolution. When a close relationship is established with God, then one will be careful not to commit mistakes and even when committed, he will take a promise not to repeat consciously. So one should think of god and the more he thinks he will imbibe the auspicious qualities of the lord as stated in the 15 chapter of The Gita, (Purushothama Prapthiyoga-The

best of all men). God consciousness will dispel the sense of ego and lead us to see and seek God everywhere. Kabirdas said that he went in search of the

love of God into the world and he found the love at all places and he felt, he experienced that and he became one in the love of God and dived in that love. This is the unselfish love made for the sake of love only. It makes man broad minded and develop sacrificial nature. God's name itself will nullify the sin as it is the embodiment of light and power. Just as water purifies the body, good thoughts purify the mind. One must become perfect and only a perfect man can influence the world. One must become a man of integrity and only he is believed, trusted and befriended by all. One can attain that purity, integrity, perfection and selflessness only by checking himself time to time his conduct, character, word, thought, deed, behavior, truthfulness and fearlessness, compassion to his fellow beings and above all absolute trust in God.

According to lord one must adopt one's own dharma and follow that culture only for his good. Adopting other dharmas or the culture which is not ours will not do any good but on the contrary, ruin him totally. "Swadharmeni Dhanam Sreyaha, Paradharmo Bhayavaha".

Woman wearing a sari which is our dharma and covering her body commands respect otherwise has to demand respect.

Ours is a Thyaga Bhoomi. One has to renunciate or sacrifice for the good of humanity otherwise bad consequences arise by lust and greed.

Man is barely 6 feet but his ambition is thousands of feet which is over ambition.

Ambition is not wrong as long as it is fair and limited.

Man has surpassed in knowledge but had not got that correlative wisdom. Man may be very great in science and technology but he must not forget that he is made up of the five elements of nature i.e. Ether, Water, Fire, Air and Sky. He must not forget that he is ruled by a known power which is unseen. He is trying to conquer the world but unable to conquer himself. If he can conquer himself, he can know himself.

Sir Arthur Eddington said of god, "You would not have found me if you had not know me". It means that every one knows that there is god which is the unknown power driving him. He maybe Asthik or Nasthik.

One must realize that God is not only in a temple/ church or a mosque. He is not confined to a particular place like a temple or a pooja room or a corner. He is at all places and at all times. Pooja or worship is not what we perform everyday at a particular time. That pooja will be confined and so God also will be confined which is not the nature of God. The worship must be continual action. Which one must experience every minute and every second. The glances that we cast from the time we get up till we sleep is the "Abhishekam" to the lord. The speech, talk, songs, hum etc that we make from morning to night is the "Stotram" to the lord. The works or actions that we perform from morning till night are the different steps or rituals performed in pooja. The distance that we walk or cover from morning till night is the "Pradakshina" to the lord. The humble "Namaskaram" with folded hands is the submission to the lord. We offer something to the lord and then take as Prasad. But what can we offer to the all-pervading lord? He is "Anantha" means "Everlasting" or "Never ending". If he really happens to take what we offer, how much can we give and how much is sufficient? So for the "Anantha Atma", we should offer our own "Atma" or "Self" which is called "Atma Nivedan" and thus submit ourselves at his holy feet. We can see Him in the sick, the disabled, the destitute etc who are otherwise called as "Daridra Narayana" according to swami Vivekananda. If we can serve them, it is the service rendered to the lord as the saying goes "Service to man is service to God"

The ideal themes of the four yogas in the Bhagavadgita as stated by God are:

The Gnana Yoga:

It is full of knowledge and wisdom. The knowledge of the ever pervading Atma not woven with the gross body. It dwells in the body but does not get attached to the body and its actions but remains by itself for itself of itself. One must feel that though he lives in the world which is full of illusions, he must do his duty, his mind with the thought "Aham Brahmasmi" means he is that Brahma and there is no difference between That and him.(That means the lord)

The Karma Yoga:

It tells that one must perform karmas or actions as decreed by God. But all the actions should be offered to god as oblation. One can offer only good actions to god as god is too good and so by performing good actions one can attain perfection of mind, heart and soul.

The Bhakti Yoga:

It tells that one must be devoted to god. It means one must trust that everything will happen on the will of god and by the grace of god. One must have a love towards god like that of a child to his mother. One must always think of god, hear his stories, praise his greatness and be peaceful and balanced in talk, action, thought and be pure in mind. His thought, word and action must be one.

The Vairagya Yoga:

It is otherwise called as the renunciation yoga. It tells that a man must renounce everything. Must sacrifice everything and surrender to the lord at his holy feet to get the salvation at the end." Sarva Dharman Parithyajya, Mamekam Saranam Vraja. Aham Thwa Sarva Papebhyo, Moksha Ishyami Masucha" Leaving all dharmas, one must take refuge at his lotus feet to attain his Pada Padmam in the end and thus get free of the birth and death cycle.

The vital chapter in the Bhagavad gita which everyone must practice are the qualities of god as described in the " Divasura Sampadvi Bhaga Yoga ".

The qualities of Daiva which are to be practised : One must practice and inculcate in them the qualities of daiva or God like ahimsa or nonviolence, truthfulness, not to be short tempered and get angry for everything, sacrifice, peace and balanced, humility, compassion towards fellow beings, pure in body and mind, selflessness, and forgiveness.

The qualities of Asura or demon which are to be discarded : One must discard the arrogance, ignorance, anger, passion, laziness, selfishness, greed, lust, impatience, intolerance, over ambition, Asatya, egoism, violence and harshness in thought, word and actions which are the qualities of Asura-demon. All this is not impossible but difficult. Hence one should pave a path for continual approach towards perfection and try to get the perfection. Once he becomes perfect, he can never become imperfect, just as a stone changed into a diamond can not become stone again.

One must cultivate humility which is the virtue of a cultured man. One must learn to obey elders, teachers, and abide by the Sastras, Vedas, Scriptures, Ethics and above all the Creation and the Creator. One must feel in the innermost that he has come into the world to discharge his duties and he is only a tool in the hands of the lord and he must endure his life to the end. Ultimately one can reach god with any of the four yogas according to his wish and convenience. One must surrender everything to the lord and seek his refuge keeping in mind that he is the savior of the clutches of samsara. The lord himself proclaimed and made Arjuna, the representative for the entire mankind, promise that the lord would give salvation to all those who trust him and also to all those who read a chapter, few verses, a verse or at least a line of the sacred book, The Bhagavadgita. Just as all the paths lead to the same goal, all the Yogas in the divine, celestial book will lead to realize the lord and reach his pada padmam in the end.

-------OM TAT SAT-------